Diabetes an

Cookbook For Seniors

Delicious Recipes to Improve Blood Sugar Control While Promoting Cardiovascular Health for Older People

Dr. Tate Mandara

Table of Contents

INTRODUCTION

Donald, a spry senior, had long battled high blood pressure and fluctuating blood sugar levels. Frustration often overshadowed his golden years, until one day, he stumbled upon this "Diabetes and Heart-Healthy Cookbook for Seniors." Skeptical but determined, Donald delved into the cookbook's pages. He embraced its breakfast recipes, savoring hearty oatmeal delights and berry bliss smoothies. Lunch became a delightful affair with chickpea salads and quinoa stir-fries. Dinners transformed into gourmet experiences as he relished grilled salmon and roasted garlic tilapia. And snacks? They were no longer forbidden; instead, he enjoyed guilt-free cucumber slices with hummus.

Slowly, Donald's health began to shift. His blood sugar levels steadied, allowing him to reduce his medications. His doctor noticed the improvement and encouraged his new culinary journey. As he continued to explore the cookbook's offerings, his high blood pressure also began to relent. Months passed, and Donald's vibrant energy returned. He felt rejuvenated, liberated from the shackles of health issues. With each recipe, he savored not just delicious meals but a newfound zest for life. This "Diabetes and Heart-Healthy Cookbook" had given him the ingredients for a healthier, more joyful chapter in his life.

Understanding Diabetes And Heart Health

Diabetes and heart health are intricately connected, sharing a complex relationship that requires a comprehensive understanding to manage and mitigate risks effectively. Diabetes, especially Type 2 diabetes, and heart disease often coexist in a potentially dangerous partnership, making it imperative to appreciate the link between them.

Diabetes - The Underlying Culprit:
Diabetes is a metabolic disorder that affects the body's ability to regulate blood sugar (glucose) levels. Uncontrolled diabetes leads to elevated blood sugar levels, which, over time, can cause damage to blood vessels and nerves. This chronic condition is a significant risk factor for cardiovascular problems.

The Link to Heart Health:
Diabetes contributes to heart issues in multiple ways. High blood sugar levels can damage blood vessels, leading to

atherosclerosis, a condition where arteries become narrow and clogged with fatty deposits. This restricts blood flow to the heart, increasing the risk of heart attacks and other cardiovascular complications.

Understanding Risk Factors:
Several risk factors exacerbate the relationship between diabetes and heart health. These include obesity, high blood pressure, high cholesterol levels, and lifestyle choices such as poor diet and lack of physical activity. Diabetes compounds these risks, creating a dangerous synergy.

Preventive Measures:
To protect heart health while living with diabetes, individuals must adopt proactive measures. Managing blood sugar through medication, diet, and exercise is crucial. A heart-healthy diet, rich in whole grains, lean

proteins, fruits, and vegetables, can significantly reduce the risk of heart disease. Regular physical activity helps control blood sugar and strengthen the heart.

The Role of Medication:

For some individuals, medication is necessary to manage diabetes and mitigate the risk of heart disease. Medications that lower blood sugar and manage blood pressure and cholesterol are commonly prescribed. Proper medication adherence, under the guidance of a healthcare professional, is vital.

Regular Monitoring and Check-Ups:

Frequent monitoring of blood sugar levels, blood pressure, and cholesterol is essential for maintaining both diabetes and heart health. Routine check-ups with healthcare providers help detect issues early and adjust treatment plans as needed. Understanding the intricate connection between diabetes and heart health is a vital step in taking control of one's well-being. With a holistic approach that encompasses healthy lifestyle choices, medication management, and regular monitoring, individuals can reduce the risks and live a fulfilling life while effectively managing both conditions.

Importance Of A Diabetes-Friendly and Healthy Diet To Seniors

The importance of a diabetes-friendly and heart-healthy diet for seniors cannot be overstated. As individuals age, they become more susceptible to health issues, and two of the most significant concerns are diabetes and heart disease.

Crafting a diet that addresses both of these conditions is paramount for seniors' overall well-being.

A diabetes-friendly diet focuses on managing blood sugar levels, a crucial consideration for seniors, as they may be dealing with Type 2 diabetes. Balanced carbohydrate intake, high-fiber foods, and lean proteins help regulate glucose levels, reducing the risk of complications. Simultaneously, a heart-healthy diet emphasizes the importance of reducing saturated fats, cholesterol, and sodium, which are common contributors to heart disease. Incorporating fruits, vegetables, whole grains, and unsaturated fats promotes cardiovascular health.

For seniors, these dietary choices offer numerous benefits.

They can help in maintaining a healthy weight, a factor that greatly influences diabetes and heart health. A well-managed diet can lead to increased energy levels and improved digestion, essential for seniors' overall vitality.

Additionally, seniors who adhere to a diabetes-friendly and heart-healthy diet may experience better blood pressure control, lowering the risk of heart-related complications. The reduced risk of blood clots, arterial plaque buildup, and inflammation is of paramount importance.

Tips for Seniors: Maintaining a Healthy Lifestyle

Maintaining a healthy lifestyle tailored to diabetes and heart health is paramount for seniors, as these conditions become more prevalent with age.

Here are some essential tips:

Nutrient-Rich Diet: A well-balanced diet is crucial for managing diabetes and heart health. Focus on whole grains, lean proteins, fiber, and heart-healthy fats like those found in nuts and avocados. Monitor carbohydrate intake to regulate blood sugar levels.

Portion Control: Watch your intake of calories by paying attention to portion sizes. Smaller, more frequent meals can lower the risk of overeating and assist in stabilizing blood sugar levels.

Regular Monitoring: Keep a close eye on blood glucose levels and blood pressure. Regular monitoring and tracking will provide insights into your health and help manage diabetes and heart conditions effectively.

Medication Adherence: If you have been prescribed medications for diabetes or heart health, follow your healthcare provider's recommendations diligently. Consistency is key to managing these conditions.

Stay Active: Engage in physical activity that suits your fitness level and health status and. Exercise helps manage blood sugar, improve cardiovascular health, and maintain overall mobility.

Hydration: Drink enough water to prevent dehydration, which can affect blood pressure and blood sugar levels.

Medication Management: If taking multiple medications, organize them with the help of a pill organizer to prevent confusion and missed doses.

Weight Management: Achieve and maintain a healthy weight because both diabetes and heart health are greatly impacted by weight management. You can get advice from your healthcare professional on how to make realistic goals.

Support System: Lean on your support system for motivation and assistance in managing your health. Joining a support group can provide invaluable insights and encouragement.

Quit Smoking: If you smoke, consider quitting. Smoking is a major risk factor for heart disease and can exacerbate diabetes-related complications.

Dental Health: Dental issues can affect heart health. Regular dental check-ups are vital to overall well-being.

By following these tailored lifestyle tips, seniors can effectively manage diabetes and heart health, ensuring a higher quality of life and greater independence in their golden years.

CHAPTER ONE

BREAKFAST RECIPES

Early Bird's Oatmeal Delight

Serving: 1
Cooking Time: 10 minutes

Ingredients:
- 1/2 cup rolled oats
- 1 cup unsweetened almond milk
- 1 small apple, diced
- 1/4 teaspoon ground cinnamon
- 1 tablespoon chopped nuts (e.g., almonds or walnuts)
- 1 teaspoon honey or a sugar-free alternative (optional)

Method of Preparation:

1. In a saucepan, combine rolled oats and almond milk.

2. Heat over medium heat, stirring occasionally, until the oats are tender and the mixture thickens (about 5-7 minutes).

3. Remove from heat and stir in diced apples and ground cinnamon.

4. Transfer the oatmeal to a serving bowl.

5. Top with chopped nuts and a drizzle of honey, if desired.

Nutritional Value (Approximate):
Calories: 300
Carbohydrates: 55g
Protein: 7g
Fiber: 10g

Healthy Fats: 8g

Sugars: 15g

Scrambled Egg Whites with Veggies

Serving: 1

Cooking Time: 15 minutes

Ingredients:

•3 egg whites

•1/4 cup diced bell peppers (red and green)

•1/4 cup diced onions

•1/4 cup diced tomatoes

•Cooking spray or a small amount of olive oil

•Salt and pepper to taste

•Fresh herbs for garnish (optional)

Method of Preparation:

1. Cooking spray or a small amount of olive oil should be lightly applied to a non-stick pan before heating it on medium heat.

2. Add the diced vegetables and cook for 3–4 minutes, or until they are cooked.

3. Salt and pepper the egg whites after whipping them in a basin until they are foamy.

4. Add the egg whites to the sautéed veggies and gently scramble for 3 to 4 minutes, or until the egg whites are done.

5. If preferred, serve hot with fresh herbs as a garnish.

Nutritional Value (Approximate):
Calories: 100

Protein: 15g

Carbohydrates: 5g

Fiber: 1g

Healthy Fats: 2g

Berry Bliss Smoothie

Serving: 1
Cooking Time: 5 minutes

Ingredients:
• 1/2 cup mixed berries (strawberries, blueberries, raspberries)
• 1/2 cup unsweetened Greek yogurt
• 1/2 cup unsweetened almond milk
• 1 tablespoon chia seeds
• 1/2 teaspoon honey or a sugar-free alternative (optional)

Method of Preparation:

1. Place the mixed berries, Greek yogurt, almond milk, and chia seeds in a blender.

2. Blend until smooth and well combined.

3. Taste and add honey if extra sweetness is desired.

4. Pour into a glass and enjoy.

Nutritional Value (Approximate):
Calories: 230
Protein: 15g
Carbohydrates: 25g
Fiber: 7g
Healthy Fats: 7g
Sugars: 12g

Whole-wheat pancakes with Berries

Serving: 1
Cooking Time: 15 minutes

Ingredients:

- 1/3 cup whole-wheat flour
- 1/2 teaspoon baking powder
- 1/4 cup unsweetened almond milk
- 1/4 teaspoon vanilla extract
- 1/4 cup mixed berries (blueberries, strawberries)
- Cooking spray or a small amount of olive oil

Method of Preparation:

1. In a mixing bowl, combine whole-wheat flour and baking powder.

2. Add almond milk and vanilla extract, and stir until a smooth batter forms.

3. Cooking spray or a little amount of olive oil should be lightly applied to a non-stick pan before heating it up on medium heat.

4. To make a pancake, pour a ladle of pancake batter onto the griddle.

5. Cook for about two minutes, or until the edges are firm and surface bubbles develop. Cook for an additional 1-2 minutes after flipping.

Nutritional Value (Approximate):

Calories: 220

Protein: 6g

Carbohydrates: 40g

Fiber: 7g

Healthy Fats: 4g

Sugars: 3g

Hard-Boiled Eggs

Serving: 1
Cooking Time: 15 minutes

Ingredients:
2 large eggs

Method of Preparation:

1. Place the eggs in a pot and cover with water.

2. Water is brought to a boil.

3. Simmer for 10–12 minutes on a lower heat.

4. Remove the eggs from heat and immediately transfer them to a bowl of ice water for a few minutes.

5. Peel and enjoy the hard-boiled eggs.
Nutritional Value (Approximate):
Calories: 140
Protein: 12g
Carbohydrates: 1g
Healthy Fats: 10g

Nutty Banana Breakfast Muffins

Serving: 1
Cooking Time: 25 minutes

Ingredients:
• 1 ripe banana, mashed
• 1/2 cup almond flour

•1/4 cup chopped nuts (e.g., walnuts or almonds)

•1/4 teaspoon baking soda

•1/4 teaspoon vanilla extract

•1 egg

•A drizzle of honey or a sugar-free alternative (optional)

Method of Preparation:

1. Paper liners should be used to line a muffin tin while your oven is preheated to 350°F (175°C).

2. Banana puree, almond flour, chopped almonds, baking soda, vanilla essence, and an egg should all be combined in a bowl.

3. Combine thoroughly after mixing.

4. In the muffin cups, distribute the mixture.

5. Bake muffins for 20 to 25 minutes, or until they are firm and well-browned.

6. Drizzle with honey if extra sweetness is desired.

Nutritional Value (Approximate):
Calories: 320
Protein: 10g
Carbohydrates: 25g
Fiber: 4g
Healthy Fats: 22g
Sugars: 11g

Spinach and Mushroom Omelet

Serving: 1
Cooking Time: 15 minutes

Ingredients:

•2 eggs

•1/4 cup chopped spinach

•1/4 cup sliced mushrooms

•1/4 cup diced bell peppers (red and green)

•1/4 cup diced onions

•Cooking spray or a small amount of olive oil

•Salt and pepper to taste

Method of Preparation:

1. Salt and pepper the eggs in a bowl after whisking them until they are foamy.

2. Cooking spray or a little amount of olive oil should be lightly applied to a non-stick pan before heating it up on medium heat.

3. Add the chopped vegetables and cook for 3–4 minutes, or until they are soft.

4. When the eggs are ready (approximately 3–4 minutes), pour them over the sautéed vegetables.

5. Serve the heated omelet folded in half.

Nutritional Value (Approximate):
Calories: 180
Protein: 14g
Carbohydrates: 7g
Fiber: 2g
Healthy Fats: 11g

CHAPTER TWO

LUNCH RECIPES

Hearty Chickpea Salad

Serving: 1
Cooking Time: 15 minutes

Ingredients:
• 1 cup canned chickpeas, drained and rinsed
• 1 cup diced cucumbers
• 1 cup cherry tomatoes, halved
• 1/4 cup diced red onions
• 1/4 cup crumbled feta cheese (optional)
• 2 tablespoons olive oil
• 1 tablespoon red wine vinegar
• Salt and pepper to taste
• Fresh herbs (e.g., parsley or basil) for garnish (optional)

Method of Preparation:

1. Combine chickpeas, cucumbers, cherry tomatoes, and red onions in a bowl.

2. In a separate small bowl, whisk together olive oil, red wine vinegar, salt, and pepper.

3. Toss the salad with the dressing after drizzling it over it.

4. Top with crumbled feta cheese and fresh herbs if desired.

Nutritional Value (Approximate):

Calories: 400

Protein: 15g

Carbohydrates: 50g

Fiber: 12g

Healthy Fats: 18g

Sugars: 8g

Grilled Chicken and Veggie Wrap

Serving: 1

Cooking Time: 20 minutes

Ingredients:

•4 ounces grilled chicken breast, sliced

•1 whole-grain tortilla

•1/2 cup mixed grilled vegetables (e.g., bell peppers, zucchini)

•2 tablespoons hummus

•Fresh greens (e.g., spinach or arugula)

•1 teaspoon olive oil

•Salt and pepper to taste

Method of Preparation:

1. Lay the whole-grain tortilla flat and spread hummus evenly over it.

2. Layer the tortilla with grilled chicken, mixed grilled vegetables, and fresh greens.

3. Toss the salad with the dressing after drizzling it over it.

4. Roll up the tortilla into a wrap and serve.

Nutritional Value (Approximate):

Calories: 350

Protein: 30g

Carbohydrates: 30g

Fiber: 7g

Healthy Fats: 12g

Quinoa and Vegetable Stir-Fry

Serving: 1

Cooking Time: 25 minutes

Ingredients:

•1/2 cup cooked quinoa

- 1/2 cup mixed stir-fry vegetables (e.g., broccoli, bell peppers, snap peas)
- 3 ounces firm tofu, cubed
- 1 tablespoon low-sodium soy sauce
- 1/2 tablespoon sesame oil
- 1/2 teaspoon minced garlic
- 1/2 teaspoon minced ginger
- 1 teaspoon chopped green onions (optional)

Method of Preparation:

1. In a skillet, heat sesame oil over medium heat and add minced garlic and ginger. Sauté for about 1 minute.

2. Add tofu cubes and stir-fry for 3-4 minutes until lightly browned.

3. Add stir-fry vegetables and continue to cook for an additional 4-5 minutes.

4. Stir in cooked quinoa and low-sodium soy sauce. Cook for another 2 minutes, ensuring everything is well combined.

5. Garnish with chopped green onions if desired.

Nutritional Value (Approximate):

Calories: 350

Protein: 20g

Carbohydrates: 45g

Fiber: 6g

Healthy Fats: 10g

Turkey and Avocado Lettuce Wraps

Serving: 1

Cooking Time: 15 minutes

Ingredients:

•4 large lettuce leaves (e.g., iceberg or butter lettuce)

•4 ounces lean ground turkey

•1/4 cup diced tomatoes

•1/4 cup diced onions

•1/4 cup diced bell peppers (red and green)

•1/4 avocado, sliced

•1/2 teaspoon olive oil

1/2 teaspoon chili powder

•Salt and pepper to taste

Method of Preparation:

1. In a skillet, heat olive oil over medium heat.

2. Add diced onions and bell peppers and sauté for about 3 minutes until tender.

3. Add ground turkey and cook until browned, breaking it into crumbles as it cooks.

4. Stir in diced tomatoes and chili powder, and cook for an additional 2 minutes.

5. Spoon the turkey mixture into lettuce leaves and top with avocado slices.

6. Season with salt and pepper to taste.

Nutritional Value (Approximate):
Calories: 350
Protein: 25g
Carbohydrates: 15g
Fiber: 6g
Healthy Fats: 18g

Tuna Salad with a Twist

Serving: 1
Cooking Time: 10 minutes

Ingredients:

- 1 can (5 ounces) tuna in water, drained
- 1/4 cup plain Greek yogurt
- 1/4 cup diced cucumber
- 1/4 cup diced red onions
- 1/4 cup diced celery
- 1/2 teaspoon lemon juice
- Salt and pepper to taste
- Lettuce leaves for serving

Method of Preparation:

1. Combine drained tuna, plain Greek yogurt, diced cucumber, red onions, and celery in a bowl.

2. Add lemon juice, salt, and pepper to taste, and mix until well combined. Serve!

Nutritional Value (Approximate):
Calories: 250
Protein: 30g
Carbohydrates: 10g

Fiber: 2g

Healthy Fats: 8g

Spinach and Quinoa Stuffed Peppers

Serving: 1

Cooking Time: 40 minutes

Ingredients:

•1 large red bell pepper

•1/4 cup cooked quinoa

•1/4 cup diced tomatoes

•1/4 cup cooked and crumbled lean ground turkey

•1/4 cup chopped spinach

•1/4 teaspoon minced garlic

•1/4 teaspoon dried basil

•1/4 teaspoon dried oregano

•Salt and pepper to taste

Method of Preparation:

1. Preheat your oven to 350°F (175°C).

2. Remove the membranes and seeds from the red bell pepper by cutting off the top.

3. Mix cooked quinoa, diced tomatoes, cooked lean ground turkey, chopped spinach, minced garlic, dried basil, dried oregano, salt, and pepper in a bowl.

4. Stuff the mixture into the bell pepper.

5. Place the stuffed pepper in an oven-safe dish and bake for about 30-35 minutes until the pepper is tender and the filling is heated through.

Nutritional Value (Approximate):
Calories: 300
Protein: 20g

Carbohydrates: 35g

Fiber: 9g

Healthy Fats: 7g

Lentil and Vegetable Soup

Serving: 1

Cooking Time: 30 minutes

Ingredients:

•1/2 cup dry green or brown lentils

•2 cups low-sodium vegetable broth

•1/2 cup diced carrots

•1/2 cup diced celery

•1/2 cup diced onions

•1/2 cup diced tomatoes

•1/2 teaspoon minced garlic

•1/2 teaspoon dried thyme

•Salt and pepper to taste

Method of Preparation:

1. In a soup pot, combine lentils, low-sodium vegetable broth, diced carrots, celery, onions, diced tomatoes, minced garlic, and dried thyme.

2. Bring the mixture to a boil, then reduce the heat to low, cover, and simmer for about 20-25 minutes, or until the lentils are tender.

3. Season with salt and pepper to taste. Serve the soup hot.

Nutritional Value (Approximate):

Calories: 300

Protein: 18g

Carbohydrates: 50g

Fiber: 17g

Healthy Fats: 1g

CHAPTER THREE

DINNER RECIPES

Lentil Shepherd's Pie

Serving: 1

Cooking Time: 45 minutes

Ingredients:

- 1/2 cup cooked green or brown lentils
- 1/4 cup diced carrots
- 1/4 cup diced celery
- 1/4 cup diced onions
- 1/4 cup diced tomatoes
- 1/4 cup frozen peas
- 1/2 cup mashed cauliflower or sweet
- potatoes (instead of traditional mashed potatoes)
- 1/2 teaspoon minced garlic

•1/2 teaspoon dried thyme

•Salt and pepper to taste

Method of Preparation:

1. Preheat your oven to 375°F (190°C).

2. In a skillet, sauté diced carrots, celery, onions, and minced garlic until they are tender (about 5 minutes).

3. Add cooked lentils, diced tomatoes, frozen peas, dried thyme, salt, and pepper to the skillet. Stir until well combined.

4. Transfer the lentil and vegetable mixture to a baking dish.

5. Spread the mashed cauliflower or sweet potatoes on top.

6. Bake for about 20-25 minutes until the top is lightly browned.

Nutritional Value (Approximate):
Calories: 350
Protein: 20g
Carbohydrates: 60g
Fiber: 15g
Healthy Fats: 5g

Grilled Veggie and Chicken Skewers

Serving: 1
Cooking Time: 20 minutes

Ingredients:
•4 ounces grilled chicken breast, cubed
•1/2 cup mixed grilled vegetables (e.g., bell peppers, zucchini, cherry tomatoes)
•1/2 teaspoon olive oil

•1/2 teaspoon dried oregano

•Salt and pepper to taste

Method of Preparation:

1. Preheat your grill to medium-high heat.

2. Thread the grilled chicken and mixed grilled vegetables alternately onto skewers.

3. Add salt, pepper, and dried oregano after brushing with olive oil.

4. Grill for about 10-12 minutes, turning occasionally, until the chicken is cooked through and the vegetables are tender.

Nutritional Value (Approximate):

Calories: 300

Protein: 30g

Carbohydrates: 15g

Fiber: 5g

Healthy Fats: 8g

Sheet Pan Chicken Fajitas

Serving: 1

Cooking Time: 30 minutes

Ingredients:

- 4 ounces chicken breast, sliced
- 1/2 cup bell peppers (mixed colors), sliced
- 1/2 cup onions, sliced
- 1/2 teaspoon chili powder
- 1/2 tcaspoon cumin
- 1/2 teaspoon paprika
- 1/2 teaspoon garlic powder
- 1/2 teaspoon olive oil
- Salt and pepper to taste

Method of Preparation:

1. Preheat your oven to 400°F (200°C).

2. Chicken breast, sliced bell peppers, onions, cumin, paprika, garlic powder, olive oil, salt, and pepper are all combined in a bowl.

3. Toss the ingredients until they are evenly coated.

4. On a baking sheet, spread the ingredients.

5. Roast the chicken for 20 to 25 minutes, or until it is thoroughly cooked and the vegetables are soft.

Nutritional Value (Approximate):
Calories: 300

Protein: 30g

Carbohydrates: 15g

Fiber: 4g

Healthy Fats: 6g

Roasted Garlic and Herb Tilapia

Serving: 1

Cooking Time: 20 minutes

Ingredients:

•4 ounces tilapia fillet

•1/2 teaspoon olive oil

•1/2 teaspoon dried herbs (e.g., rosemary, thyme, oregano)

•1/2 teaspoon minced garlic

•Salt and pepper to taste

Method of Preparation:

1. Preheat your oven to 375°F (190°C).

2. Mix olive oil, dried herbs, minced garlic, salt, and pepper in a small bowl

3. Place the tilapia filet on a baking sheet and brush with the herb mixture.

4. Roast for about 15-18 minutes until the tilapia flakes easily with a fork.

Nutritional Value (Approximate):
Calories: 200
Protein: 30g
Carbohydrates: 2g
Healthy Fats: 8g

Spaghetti Squash with Marinara Sauce

Serving: 1

Cooking Time: 45 minutes

Ingredients:
- 1/2 medium spaghetti squash
- 1/2 cup low-sodium marinara sauce
- 1/4 cup diced tomatoes
- 1/4 teaspoon dried basil
- 1/4 teaspoon dried oregano
- 1/4 teaspoon minced garlic
- Salt and pepper to taste

Method of Preparation:

1. Preheat your oven to 375°F (190°C).

2. Remove the seeds from the spaghetti squash by cutting it in half lengthwise.

3. Roast the squash halves for about 30-35 minutes, or until the flesh is soft, by placing them cut side down on a baking sheet.

4. With a fork, create "spaghetti" out of the cooked squash.

5. Warm the marinara sauce and stir in the diced tomatoes, dried oregano, dry basil, minced garlic, salt, and pepper.

6. Spaghetti squash should be topped with marinara sauce.

Nutritional Value (Approximate):

Calories: 250

Protein: 3g

Carbohydrates: 60g

Fiber: 15g

Healthy Fats: 2g

Broiled Flounder with Citrus Glaze

Serving: 1
Cooking Time: 15 minutes

Ingredients:
- 4 ounces flounder filet
- 1/2 teaspoon olive oil
- Juice of 1/2 lemon
- Juice of 1/2 orange
- 1/2 teaspoon honey or a sugar-free alternative
- Salt and pepper to taste
- Lemon and orange slices for garnish (optional)

Method of Preparation:

1. Preheat your broiler.

2. Whisk together olive oil, lemon juice, orange juice, honey, salt, and pepper in a small bowl

3. Brush the flounder fillet with the citrus glaze.

4. Place the filet on a broiler pan and broil for about 8-10 minutes until the fish flakes easily.

5. Garnish with lemon and orange slices if desired.

Nutritional Value (Approximate):
Calories: 200
Protein: 25g
Carbohydrates: 5g
Healthy Fats: 4g

Veggie and Bean Chili

Serving: 1

Cooking Time: 30 minutes

Ingredients:

- 1/2 cup low-sodium vegetable broth
- 1/2 cup diced tomatoes
- 1/4 cup diced onions
- 1/4 cup diced bell peppers (red and green)
- 1/4 cup diced zucchini
- 1/4 cup canned kidney beans, drained and rinsed
- 1/2 teaspoon chili powder
- 1/2 teaspoon cumin
- 1/2 teaspoon paprika
- Salt and pepper to taste

Method of Preparation:

1. In a saucepan, combine low-sodium vegetable broth, diced tomatoes, onions, bell peppers, zucchini, kidney beans, chili powder, cumin, paprika, salt, and pepper.

2. Simmer for about 20-25 minutes until the vegetables are tender and the chili has thickened. Serve hot.

Nutritional Value (Approximate):

Calories: 300

Protein: 12g

Carbohydrates: 60g

Fiber: 15g

Healthy Fats: 1g

CHAPTER FOUR

SNACK RECIPES

Whole-wheat crackers with Hummus

Serving: 1
Cooking Time: 5 minutes

Ingredients:
- 6 whole-wheat crackers
- 2 tablespoons hummus
- Sliced cucumbers, cherry tomatoes, or bell pepper strips for topping (optional)

Method of Preparation:

1. Arrange whole-wheat crackers on a plate.

2. Spread a dollop of hummus on each cracker.

3. Top with sliced cucumbers, cherry tomatoes, or bell pepper strips if desired.

Nutritional Value (Approximate):
Calories: 150
Protein: 5g
Carbohydrates: 25g
Fiber: 5g
Healthy Fats: 4g

Cucumber and Hummus Slices

Serving: 1
Cooking Time: 5 minutes

Ingredients:
•1 medium cucumber
•2 tablespoons hummus

Method of Preparation:

1. Wash and peel the cucumber, if desired.

2. Slice the cucumber into rounds.

3. Dip each cucumber slice into hummus before eating.

Nutritional Value (Approximate):

Calories: 50

Protein: 2g

Carbohydrates: 8g

Fiber: 2g

Healthy Fats: 1g

Apple Slices with Peanut Butter

Serving: 1

Cooking Time: 5 minutes

Ingredients:
- 1 medium apple, sliced
- 2 tablespoons natural peanut butter

Method of Preparation:

1. Slice the apple into wedges.

2. Serve with a side of natural peanut butter for dipping.

Nutritional Value (Approximate):

Calories: 200

Protein: 7g

Carbohydrates: 20g

Fiber: 4g

Healthy Fats: 12g

Guacamole and Whole-Grain Crackers

Serving: 1
Cooking Time: 10 minutes

Ingredients:
- 1/2 ripe avocado, mashed
- 1/4 cup diced tomatoes
- 1/4 cup diced onions
- 1/4 cup diced cilantro
- 1/2 teaspoon minced garlic
- Juice of 1/2 lime
- A pinch of salt and pepper
- 6 whole-grain crackers

Method of Preparation:

1. Combine mashed avocado, diced tomatoes, onions, cilantro, minced garlic, lime juice, salt, and pepper to make guacamole in a bowl.

2. Serve with whole-grain crackers.

Nutritional Value (Approximate):

Calories: 300

Protein: 5g

Carbohydrates: 25g

Fiber: 8g

Healthy Fats: 20g

Cottage Cheese and Pineapple Cups

Serving: 1
Cooking Time: 5 minutes

Ingredients:
•1/2 cup low-fat cottage cheese
•1/2 cup pineapple chunks (fresh or canned in juice)

Method of Preparation:

1. Combine low-fat cottage cheese and pineapple chunks in a bowl.

2. Serve in a cup or bowl.

Nutritional Value (Approximate):
Calories: 150
Protein: 15g

Carbohydrates: 20g

Fiber: 2g

Healthy Fats: 1g

Low-Fat Cheese

Serving: 1

Cooking Time: None

Ingredients:

•1 small portion of low-fat cheese (e.g., string cheese or cheese slices)

Method of Preparation:

1. Simply enjoy a small portion of low-fat cheese.

Nutritional Value (Approximate):

Calories: 50-80

Protein: 7-8g

Carbohydrates: 0-1g

Healthy Fats: 2-3g

Baked Sweet Potato Fries

Serving: 1

Cooking Time: 30 minutes

Ingredients:

- 1 small sweet potato
- 1/2 teaspoon olive oil
- 1/2 teaspoon paprika
- A pinch of salt

Method of Preparation:

1. Preheat your oven to 425°F (220°C).

2. Cut the sweet potato into thin strips to resemble fries.

3. Toss the sweet potato strips with olive oil, paprika, and a pinch of salt.

4. Spread them on a baking sheet.

5. Bake for about 20-25 minutes until they're crispy and lightly browned.

Nutritional Value (Approximate):

Calories: 150

Protein: 2g

Carbohydrates: 30g

Fiber: 5g

Healthy Fats: 2g

CHAPTER FIVE

FISH & SEAFOODS RECIPES

Lemon Garlic Shrimp Scampi

Serving: 1
Cooking Time: 15 minutes

Ingredients:
- 6 large shrimp, peeled and deveined
- 1 clove garlic, minced
- 1/2 lemon, juiced
- 1 tablespoon olive oil
- 1/4 teaspoon dried oregano
- Salt and pepper to taste
- Fresh parsley for garnish (optional)
- Whole-grain pasta or zucchini noodles for serving (optional)

Method of Preparation:

1. Olive oil should be heated in a skillet over medium heat.

2. Sauté for about a minute after adding the minced garlic.

3. Add shrimp and cook for 2-3 minutes on each side or until they turn pink.

4. Drizzle lemon juice over the shrimp, and sprinkle with dried oregano, salt, and pepper.

5. Serve hot with whole-grain pasta or zucchini noodles, and garnish with fresh parsley if desired.

Nutritional Value (Approximate):

Calories: 200

Protein: 20g

Carbohydrates: 5g

Healthy Fats: 10g

Grilled Swordfish with Herb Butter

Serving: 1

Cooking Time: 20 minutes

Ingredients:

•4 ounces swordfish steak

•1/2 teaspoon olive oil

•1/2 teaspoon dried basil

•1/2 teaspoon dried thyme

•Salt and pepper to taste

•Herb butter (mix melted unsalted butter with chopped fresh herbs) for topping

Method of Preparation:

1. Preheat your grill to medium-high heat.

2. Brush the swordfish steak with olive oil and sprinkle with dried basil, dried thyme, salt, and pepper.

3. Grill for about 4-5 minutes on each side or until the fish is opaque and flakes easily.

4. Top with herb butter before serving.

Nutritional Value (Approximate):
Calories: 250
Protein: 25g
Carbohydrates: 1g
Healthy Fats: 16g

Baked Cod with Mediterranean Salsa

Serving: 1
Cooking Time: 25 minutes

Ingredients:

•4 ounces cod fillet

•1/2 teaspoon olive oil

•1/4 cup diced tomatoes

•1/4 cup diced cucumbers

•1/4 cup diced red onions

•1/4 cup diced black olives

•1/2 lemon, juiced

•1/2 teaspoon dried oregano

•Salt and pepper to taste

Method of Preparation:

1. Preheat your oven to 375°F (190°C).

2. Brush the cod filet with olive oil and season with salt and pepper.

3. Bake for about 15-20 minutes or until the fish is opaque and flakes easily.

4. Combine diced tomatoes, cucumbers, red onions, black olives, lemon juice, dried oregano, salt, and pepper to create the Mediterranean salsa in a bowl.

5. Serve the cod topped with Mediterranean salsa.

Nutritional Value (Approximate):
Calories: 250
Protein: 20g
Carbohydrates: 10g
Fiber: 2g
Healthy Fats: 10g

Seared Tuna Steaks with Sesame Glaze

Serving: 1
Cooking Time: 10 minutes

Ingredients:

- 4 ounces of tuna steak
- 1/2 teaspoon sesame oil
- 1/2 teaspoon low-sodium soy sauce
- 1/2 teaspoon sesame seeds
- Salt and pepper to taste

Method of Preparation:

1. Sesame oil should be heated in a skillet over medium heat.

2. Season the tuna steak with salt and pepper and sear for about 2-3 minutes on each side, or until it's seared on the outside but pink in

the center.

3. Drizzle low-sodium soy sauce over the tuna steak and sprinkle with sesame seeds before serving.

Nutritional Value (Approximate):
Calories: 200
Protein: 25g
Carbohydrates: 1g
Healthy Fats: 8g

Spicy Cajun Salmon

Serving: 1
Cooking Time: 20 minutes

Ingredients:
- 4 ounces salmon fillet
- 1/2 teaspoon Cajun seasoning
- 1/2 teaspoon olive oil

•A pinch of cayenne pepper (adjust to your spice preference)

•Lemon wedges for garnish

Method of Preparation:

1. Preheat your oven to 375°F (190°C).

2. Rub olive oil over the salmon fillet.

3. Sprinkle Cajun seasoning and cayenne pepper over the salmon.

4. Bake for about 15-20 minutes or until the salmon is cooked through and flakes easily.

5. Serve with lemon wedges for garnish.

Nutritional Value (Approximate):

Calories: 250

Protein: 25g

Carbohydrates: 2g

Healthy Fats: 14g

Citrus Marinated Grilled Trout

Serving: 1

Cooking Time: 20 minutes

Ingredients:

• 4 ounces trout fillet

• Juice of 1/2 lemon

• Juice of 1/2 orange

• 1/2 teaspoon olive oil

• 1/2 teaspoon dried thyme

• Salt and pepper to taste

Method of Preparation:

1. Preheat your grill to medium-high heat.

2. Mix lemon juice, orange juice, olive oil, dried thyme, salt, and pepper in a bowl.

3. Marinate the trout fillet in the citrus mixture for about 10 minutes.

4. Grill the trout for about 4-5 minutes on each side or until it's cooked through and flakes easily.

Nutritional Value (Approximate):
Calories: 200
Protein: 25g
Carbohydrates: 4g
Healthy Fats: 8g

Miso-Glazed Mahi-Mahi

Serving: 1
Cooking Time: 15 minutes

Ingredients:
•4 ounces Mahi-Mahi fillet
•1/2 teaspoon miso paste

- 1/2 teaspoon low-sodium soy sauce
- 1/2 teaspoon honey or a sugar-free alternative
- 1/2 teaspoon minced ginger
- Sesame seeds for garnish

Method of Preparation:

1. Preheat your broiler.

2. Mix miso paste, low-sodium soy sauce, honey, and minced ginger in a bowl.

3. Brush the Mahi-Mahi fillet with the miso glaze.

4. Broil for about 7-8 minutes or until the fish is cooked through.

5. Garnish with sesame seeds before serving.

CHAPTER SIX

SOUP AND STEW RECIPES

Vegetable and Bean Minestrone

Serving: 1
Cooking Time: 30 minutes

Ingredients:
- 1/2 cup low-sodium vegetable broth
- 1/4 cup diced tomatoes
- 1/4 cup diced carrots
- 1/4 cup diced celery
- 1/4 cup diced onions
- 1/4 cup cooked kidney beans
- 1/4 cup cooked whole wheat pasta
- 1/4 teaspoon dried basil
- Salt and pepper to taste

Method of Preparation:

1. In a pot, combine low-sodium vegetable broth, diced tomatoes, carrots, celery, onions, kidney beans, and dried basil.

2. Simmer for about 20-25 minutes until the vegetables are tender.

3. Add cooked whole wheat pasta and season with salt and pepper. Serve hot.

Nutritional Value (Approximate):
Calories: 250
Protein: 10g
Carbohydrates: 45g
Fiber: 10g
Healthy Fats: 1g

Creamy Tomato Basil Soup

Serving: 1

Cooking Time: 20 minutes

Ingredients:
- 1/2 cup low-sodium tomato soup
- 1/4 cup low-fat Greek yogurt
- 1/4 teaspoon dried basil
- Salt and pepper to taste

Method of Preparation:

1. In a saucepan, combine low-sodium tomato soup, low-fat Greek yogurt, dried basil, salt, and pepper.

2. Heat over medium heat until warmed through. Serve hot.

Nutritional Value (Approximate):

Calories: 150

Protein: 10g

Carbohydrates: 20g

Fiber: 5g

Healthy Fats: 2g

Chicken and Wild Rice Soup

Serving: 1

Cooking Time: 30 minutes

Ingredients:

- 1/2 cup low-sodium chicken broth
- 4 ounces cooked chicken breast, diced
- 1/4 cup cooked wild rice
- 1/4 cup diced carrots
- 1/4 cup diced celery
- 1/4 cup diced onions

•1/4 teaspoon dried thyme

•Salt and pepper to taste

Method of Preparation:

1. In a pot, combine low-sodium chicken broth, cooked chicken breast, wild rice, carrots, celery, onions, dried thyme, salt, and pepper.

2. Simmer for about 20-25 minutes until the vegetables are tender. Serve hot.

Nutritional Value (Approximate):

Calories: 300

Protein: 30g

Carbohydrates: 30g

Fiber: 5g

Healthy Fats: 2g

Split Pea Soup

Serving: 1

Cooking Time: 45 minutes

Ingredients:
- 1/2 cup split peas
- 2 cups low-sodium vegetable broth
- 1/4 cup diced carrots
- 1/4 cup diced celery
- 1/4 cup diced onions
- 1/4 teaspoon dried thyme
- Salt and pepper to taste

Method of Preparation:

1. In a pot, combine split peas, low-sodium vegetable broth, carrots, celery, onions, dried thyme, salt, and pepper.

2. Simmer for about 35-40 minutes until the split peas are soft. Serve hot.

Nutritional Value (Approximate):
Calories: 250
Protein: 15g
Carbohydrates: 45g
Fiber: 10g
Healthy Fats: 1g

Beef and Vegetable Soup

Serving: 1
Cooking Time: 30 minutes

Ingredients:
- 1/2 cup low-sodium beef broth
- 2 ounces lean beef (such as sirloin or round steak), thinly sliced
- 1/4 cup diced carrots
- 1/4 cup diced celery

- 1/4 cup diced onions
- 1/4 teaspoon dried thyme
- Salt and pepper to taste

Method of Preparation:

1. In a pot, combine low-sodium beef broth, thinly sliced lean beef, carrots, celery, onions, dried thyme, salt, and pepper.

2. Simmer for about 20-25 minutes until the beef is cooked and the vegetables are tender. Serve hot.

Nutritional Value (Approximate):

Calories: 250

Protein: 20g

Carbohydrates: 10g

Fiber: 3g

Healthy Fats: 5g

Split Pea and Ham Hock Stew

Serving: 1

Cooking Time: 1 hour 30 minutes

Ingredients:
- 1/2 cup split peas
- 2 cups low-sodium vegetable broth
- 2 ounces lean ham hock (or lean ham), diced
- 1/4 cup diced carrots
- 1/4 cup diced celery
- 1/4 cup diced onions
- 1/4 teaspoon dried thyme
- Salt and pepper to taste

Method of Preparation:

1. In a pot, combine split peas, low-sodium vegetable broth, diced ham hock, carrots, celery, onions, dried thyme, salt, and pepper.

2. Simmer for about 1 hour until the split peas are soft and the ham is tender. Serve hot.

Nutritional Value (Approximate):
Calories: 300
Protein: 20g
Carbohydrates: 40g
Fiber: 15g
Healthy Fats: 5g

Butternut Squash and Apple Bisque

Serving: 1
Cooking Time: 30 minutes

Ingredients:
- 1/2 cup low-sodium vegetable broth
- 1/2 cup diced butternut squash
- 1/2 cup diced apples

- 1/4 cup diced onions
- 1/4 teaspoon cinnamon
- Salt and pepper to taste
- Greek yogurt for topping (optional)

Method of Preparation:

1. In a pot, combine low-sodium vegetable broth, diced butternut squash, apples, onions, cinnamon, salt, and pepper.

2. Simmer for about 20-25 minutes until the squash and apples are tender.

3. Use a blender or immersion blender to blend until thoroughly smooth.

4. Serve hot and top with a dollop of Greek yogurt if desired.

Nutritional Value (Approximate):

Calories: 200

Protein: 4g

Carbohydrates: 45g

Fiber: 8g

Healthy Fats: 1g

CHAPTER SEVEN

DESSERT RECIPES

Angel Food Cake with Berries

Serving: 1
Preparation Time: 10 minutes

Ingredients:
• 1 slice of angel food cake
• 1/2 cup mixed berries (strawberries, blueberries, raspberries)
• A dollop of Greek yogurt or a sugar-free whipped topping (optional)

Method of Preparation:

1. An angel food cake slice should be placed on a platter.

2. Top it with mixed berries.

3. Add a dollop of Greek yogurt or a sugar-free whipped topping if desired.

Nutritional Value (Approximate):
Calories: 150
Protein: 3g
Carbohydrates: 35g
Fiber: 5g
Healthy Fats: 0.5g

Baked Apples with Cinnamon

Serving: 1
Preparation Time: 40 minutes

Ingredients:
•1 medium apple
•1/2 teaspoon cinnamon
•A sprinkle of nutmeg (optional)

•A small drizzle of honey or a sugar-free alternative (optional)

Method of Preparation:

1. Preheat your oven to 350°F (175°C).

2. Wash and core the apple.

3. Place the apple in an oven-safe dish.

4. Sprinkle with cinnamon and nutmeg, and drizzle with honey if desired.

5. Bake for about 30-35 minutes until the apple is tender.

Nutritional Value (Approximate):
Calories: 100
Protein: 0.5g
Carbohydrates: 25g

Fiber: 4g

Healthy Fats: 0.5g

Berry Parfait with Greek Yogurt

Serving: 1

Preparation Time: 5 minutes

Ingredients:

•1/2 cup mixed berries (strawberries, blueberries, raspberries)

•1/2 cup low-fat Greek yogurt

•A sprinkle of granola (optional)

Method of Preparation:

1. In a glass or bowl, layer mixed berries and low-fat Greek yogurt.

2. Add a sprinkle of granola if desired.

Nutritional Value (Approximate):

Calories: 150

Protein: 10g

Carbohydrates: 20g

Fiber: 5g

Healthy Fats: 2g

Dark Chocolate-Dipped Strawberries

Serving: 1

Preparation Time: 15 minutes

Ingredients:

•3-4 fresh strawberries

•1 square of dark chocolate (70% cocoa or higher)

Method of Preparation:

1. Wash and dry the strawberries.

2. Melt the dark chocolate square using a double boiler or in the microwave.

3. Dip the strawberries into the melted dark chocolate, covering half or all of the strawberries as desired.

4. To allow the chocolate to harden, place it on parchment paper.

Nutritional Value (Approximate):
Calories: 100
Protein: 1g
Carbohydrates: 10g
Fiber: 2g
Healthy Fats: 6g

Lemon Sorbet with Fresh Berries

Serving: 1
Preparation Time: 5 minutes

Ingredients:
• 1 scoop of lemon sorbet
• 1/2 cup mixed berries (strawberries, blueberries, raspberries)

Method of Preparation:

1. Place a scoop of lemon sorbet in a dish.

2. Top it with mixed berries. Serve

Nutritional Value (Approximate):
Calories: 150
Protein: 1g
Carbohydrates: 35g

Fiber: 3g

Healthy Fats: 0.5g

Pumpkin Pie (Sugar-Free)

Serving: 1

Preparation Time: 30 minutes

Ingredients:

•1 small slice of sugar-free pumpkin pie

Method of Preparation:

1. Serve a small slice of sugar-free pumpkin pie.

Nutritional Value (Approximate):

Calories: 100

Protein: 1g

Carbohydrates: 20g

Fiber: 2g

Healthy Fats: 3g

Frozen Yogurt

Serving: 1
Preparation Time: 5 minutes

Ingredients:
•1/2 cup low-fat frozen yogurt (sugar-free or no-sugar-added)

Method of Preparation:

1. Serve a scoop of low-fat frozen yogurt.

Nutritional Value (Approximate):
Calories: 100
Protein: 3g
Carbohydrates: 20g
Healthy Fats: 2g

7-DAY MEAL PLAN

Day 1

Breakfast: Berry Bliss Smoothie
Lunch: Hearty Chickpea Salad
Dinner: Lentil Shepherd's Pie
Snack: Whole-wheat crackers with Hummus

Day 2

Breakfast: Scrambled Egg Whites with Veggies
Lunch: Quinoa and Vegetable Stir-Fry
Dinner: Grilled Swordfish with Herb Butter
Snack: Apple Slices with Peanut Butter

Day 3

Breakfast: Nutty Banana Breakfast Muffins

Lunch: Lentil and Vegetable Soup

Dinner: Sheet Pan Chicken Fajitas

Snack: Guacamole and Whole-Grain Crackers

Day 4

Breakfast: Whole-wheat pancakes with Berries

Lunch: Tuna Salad with a Twist

Dinner: Spaghetti Squash with Marinara Sauce

Snack: Low-Fat Cheese

Day 5

Breakfast: Hard-Boiled Eggs

Lunch: Spinach and Quinoa Stuffed Peppers

Dinner: Spicy Cajun Salmon

Snack: Baked Sweet Potato Fries

Day 6

Breakfast: Early Bird's Oatmeal Delight
Lunch: Grilled Chicken and Veggie Wrap
Dinner: Citrus Marinated Grilled Trout
Snack: Cucumber and Hummus Slices

Day 7

Breakfast: Spinach and Mushroom Omelette
Lunch: Lentil and Vegetable Soup
Dinner: Miso-Glazed Mahi-Mahi
Snack: Dark Chocolate-Dipped Strawberries

This 7-day meal plan combines a variety of delicious and heart-healthy recipes for a well-rounded diet. Remember to adjust portion sizes to meet your specific dietary needs. Enjoy your meals!

CONCLUSION

In the pages of this Diabetes and Heart Healthy Cookbook for Seniors, we've embarked on a journey toward better health, improved well-being, and a happier life. Through carefully crafted recipes and expert guidance, we've explored the world of diabetes-friendly and heart-healthy cuisine, proving that health-conscious eating can also be a delightful culinary experience. Our journey has taken us through the chapters of wholesome breakfasts, nourishing lunches, satisfying dinners, revitalizing snacks, delectable fish and seafood delights, comforting soups and stews, and mouthwatering desserts.

We've found that maintaining heart health and controlling diabetes don't need giving up flavor or enjoyment.

But beyond these recipes, we've discovered a more profound truth: You can take charge of your health. By following this diet, you're empowering yourself while also nourishing your body. Every dish you make from this cookbook is a step in the direction of living a healthier, more energetic life. Living is more important than just eating. This cookbook is proof that maintaining good health should not be a cause for mourning. It's a celebration of the life you deserve, one unrestricted by diabetes and cardiovascular problems.

So, as you turn the final pages of this cookbook, I encourage you to take these recipes to heart and make them a part of your daily life. Embrace this lifestyle with a newfound zeal, for the journey doesn't end here. The key to lasting health and vitality is to make this cookbook a constant companion, a guiding light on your path to a life filled with energy, joy, and health. I believe in your strength and determination to prioritize your well-being. Every meal you prepare from this cookbook is a choice—a choice for a healthier, happier, and more fulfilling life. Embrace it, savor it, and live it. Your health is your greatest wealth, and this cookbook is your invaluable tool on the path to that treasure.

Made in United States
Troutdale, OR
12/23/2024

27211480R00064